PORT LOCKROY
Goudier Island, Antarctica
Photo by Kevin Fohrer

AWA
ACCIDENTALLY WES ANDERSON

STAMP

Less than two thousand miles from the South Pole, the Penguin Post Office is the most visited site on the continent. The staff of four processes seventy thousand pieces of mail sent by intrepid travelers during the five-month Antarctic season.

HOTEL OPERA
Prague, Czech Republic
Photo by Valentina Jacks

AWA

ACCIDENTALLY WES ANDERSON

STAMP

A hot-pink confection of Bohemian Neo-Renaissance style, the Hotel Opera stands in the less touristy New Town quarter of Prague...which, contrary to its name, is not particularly near the opera.

GREAT MARKET HALL
Budapest, Hungary
Photo by Marcus Cederberg

AWA
ACCIDENTALLY WES ANDERSON

STAMP

This market shines like a beacon, thanks to its unmistakable roof of iridescent multicolored tiles made by the famed Zsolnay ceramics factory in Pécs.

SLOVENIAN RAILWAYS

Pragersko, Slovenia

Photo by Nastja Kikec

AWA

ACCIDENTALLY WES ANDERSON

STAMP

The sleek modern trains of Slovenia's national rail service represent just one chapter in a sequence of dramatic changes that the country has undergone.

HOTEL
GLETSCHER - RESTAURANT
BELVEDERE

HOTEL BELVÉDÈRE
Furka Pass, Switzerland
Photo by Carlo Küttel

AWA
ACCIDENTALLY WES ANDERSON

STAMP

Cradled by a hairpin turn on a dramatic, winding road in the Swiss Alps, this hotel served as the backdrop to a memorable scene in the James Bond film *Goldfinger*.

LIFEGUARD CHAIR
ON LAKE LLANQUIHUE

Frutillar, Chile

Photo by Jaime Kunstmann

AWA

ACCIDENTALLY WES ANDERSON

STAMP

Home to around fifteen thousand residents, Frutillar not only borders the largest lake entirely within Chile but also has the honor of being recognized as the country's first UNESCO Creative City of Music.

ACKERMAN
BLUE MARLIN

SKYLINE
Willemstad, Curaçao
Photo by Jeffrey Czum

AWA
ACCIDENTALLY WES ANDERSON

STAMP

Though it is located in the southern Caribbean Sea, Curaçao is actually a "constituent country" of the Kingdom of the Netherlands. The island is also home to an incredible blend of cultures, thanks to its complex, layered history.

LES ÉCLAIREURS LIGHTHOUSE
Ushuaia, Argentina
Photo by Bianca Berti

AWA
ACCIDENTALLY WES ANDERSON

STAMP

This hundred-year-old lighthouse is located on a rocky inlet at the southernmost tip of South America—an area known as the "End of the World."

LES CHEMINS DE FER DU SENEGAL
DEPART
GARE DE DAKAR
ARRIVEE

DAKAR RAILWAY STATION

Dakar, Senegal

Photo by Sheryl Cababa

AWA

ACCIDENTALLY WES ANDERSON

STAMP

For a time, the return to regular passenger service at Dakar's candy-colored railway station seemed unlikely, but thanks to restoration efforts and a fresh coat of paint, trains are once again running. All aboard!

STOP

MURDEIRA
Sal, Cape Verde
Photo by Aude Olesen

AWA
ACCIDENTALLY WES ANDERSON

STAMP

Discovered in 1460, Sal is one of the ten islands of Cape Verde, an archipelago off the coast of West Africa. Its name was revised to Sal (the Portuguese word for "salt") when two large deposits were found here.

CAMEL CROSSING
Masada National Park, Israel
Photo by Andrew Weaver

AWA
ACCIDENTALLY WES ANDERSON

STAMP

Nicknamed "ships of the desert," camels at this UNESCO world heritage site are ridden almost exclusively by tourists—an ill-advised attraction for those who struggle with motion sickness.

GLENORCHY

WHARF SHED

Glenorchy, South Island,
New Zealand
Photo by Frida Berg

AWA
ACCIDENTALLY WES ANDERSON

STAMP

For nearly a century, the only access to Glenorchy was by steamboat, and this shed served as the sole site for arrivals and departures.

WHS

HOT-AIR BALLOON
Hamilton, North Island,
New Zealand
Photo by Marie Valencia

AWA
ACCIDENTALLY WES ANDERSON

STAMP

When hot-air balloons were first tested, farmers believed they were aliens descending from the sky to land in their fields. To allay their fears, pilots would share a bottle of champagne with them. Thus, a tradition was born. Cheers!

PUSH
PUSH
1

JAPAN RAILWAYS
Tokyo, Japan
Photo by AccidentallyWesAnderson

AWA
ACCIDENTALLY WES ANDERSON

STAMP

While punctuality is a well-known tenet of Japanese travel, a lesser-known aspect is the trainspotters—and the dozens of corresponding official titles they hold. Our favorite? *Ekiben-tetsu,* fanatics of the bento boxes sold at said stations.

ASCENSOR DA BICA
Lisbon, Portugal
Photo by Jack Spicer Adams

AWA
ACCIDENTALLY WES ANDERSON

STAMP

The Ascensor da Bica climbs one of Lisbon's steepest hills—a terrace at the top provides views of the distinct rooftops of Europe's westernmost capital city.

THE ECONOMICAL SHOE STORE
E^{LE} AZZOPARDI
95

THE ECONOMICAL SHOE STORE

Valletta, Malta

Photo by Michael Hsieh

STAMP

After traversing Valletta's twisting alleys, you'll be relieved to find this storefront and a fresh pair of soles to carry you forward on your adventure.

HÚSAVÍK LIGHTHOUSE
Húsavík, Iceland
Photo by Matthijs Van Mierlo

AWA

ACCIDENTALLY WES ANDERSON

STAMP

This brilliantly painted lighthouse shines bright on the coast of Iceland—and offers a perfect vantage point from which to witness the aurora borealis light up the sky.

COCOA
MILK
SUGAR

MALLEY'S CHOCOLATES
Cleveland, Ohio
Photo by AccidentallyWesAnderson

AWA
ACCIDENTALLY WES ANDERSON

STAMP

Each perfectly pink eighty-eight-foot silo holds roughly a hundred thousand pounds of the respective raw ingredients that make Malley's chocolate so delicious.

JOYCE

JOYCE THEATER
New York, New York
Photo by Jessica Hriniak

AWA

ACCIDENTALLY WES ANDERSON

STAMP

In 1970 the "midnight movie" was invented here when a Polish immigrant played a surrealist western to a sold-out house seven nights a week for six months straight.

WARRENDER BATHS CLUB
Edinburgh, Scotland
Photo by Soo Burnell

AWA

ACCIDENTALLY WES ANDERSON

STAMP

Utilized for more than leisure, this famed swimming club has seen its fair share of Olympic medalists train in these lanes.

GRÖNA LUND
Stockholm, Sweden
Photo by Marta Rękas

AWA
ACCIDENTALLY WES ANDERSON

STAMP

Sweden's oldest amusement park is a "magical world where the impossible becomes possible. Old gets young, little gets big, up gets down and down gets up," according to official descriptions.

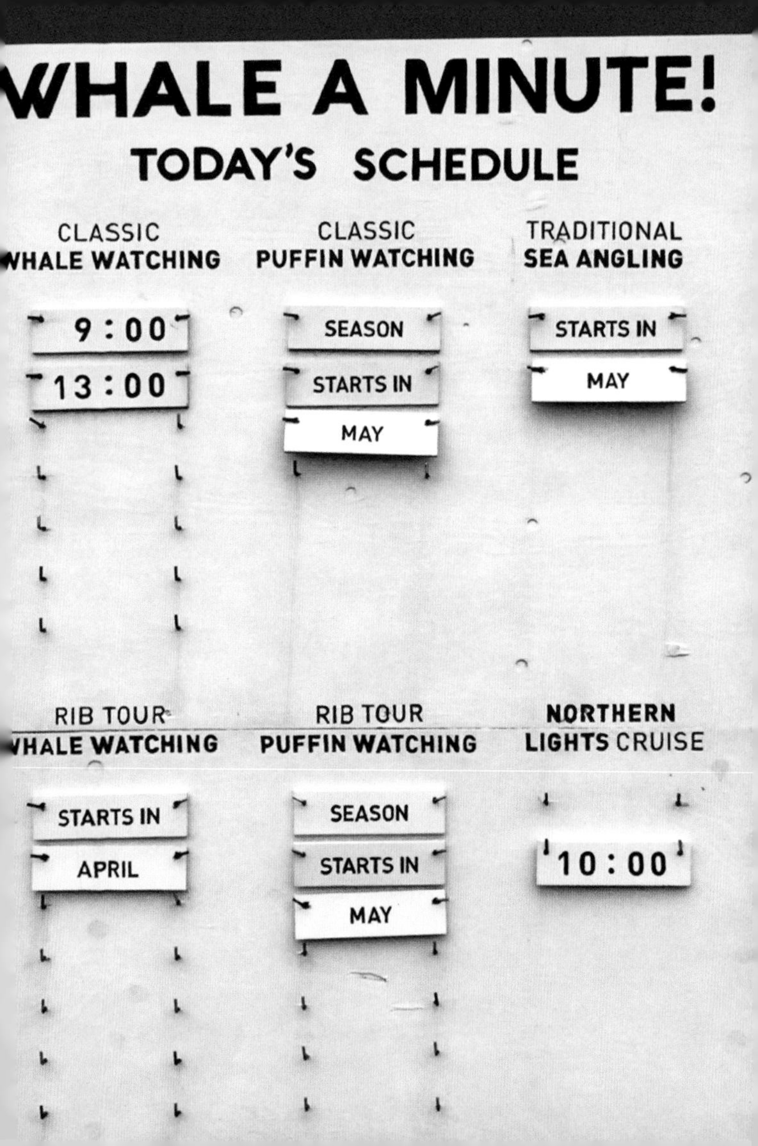

WHALE A MINUTE!

TODAY'S SCHEDULE

CLASSIC WHALE WATCHING	CLASSIC PUFFIN WATCHING	TRADITIONAL SEA ANGLING
9:00	SEASON	STARTS IN
13:00	STARTS IN	MAY
	MAY	

RIB TOUR WHALE WATCHING	RIB TOUR PUFFIN WATCHING	NORTHERN LIGHTS CRUISE
STARTS IN	SEASON	10:00
APRIL	STARTS IN	
	MAY	

REYKJAVÍK OLD HARBOUR
Reykjavík, Iceland
Photo by Keira Lyons

AWA
ACCIDENTALLY WES ANDERSON

STAMP

Home to descendants of Viking settlers, Iceland also plays host to a healthy marine ecosystem. Each year, from April to August, half the world's population of Atlantic puffins settles on tiny offshore islands in search of a mate.

H593
XWW

FIGARO
South Yorkshire, England
Photo by Hayley Doyle

AWA
ACCIDENTALLY WES ANDERSON

STAMP

This happy little two-door convertible was conceived by a fashion designer who had never designed a car and didn't even have a driver's license. It's been said that "If you can't parallel park the Figaro, you should be walking."

101
POSTMASTER
TRADING POST

POST OFFICE
Wrangell, Alaska
Photo by Robin Petravic
and Catherine Bailey

AWA

ACCIDENTALLY WES ANDERSON

STAMP

The citizens of Wrangell once rejected a proposal for standard mail-delivery service—they much prefer the social ritual of visiting the post office in person.

PLAYA LOS ÓRGANOS

Piura, Peru

Photo by Matías De Caro

AWA

ACCIDENTALLY WES ANDERSON

STAMP

Once home to record-breaking big-game fishing, today this secluded beach town is a haven for "smaller game" local fishermen and -women.

VIEWFINDER
Monopoli, Italy
Photo by Ky Allport

AWA

ACCIDENTALLY WES ANDERSON

STAMP

Panoramic telescopes provide a magnified view from the port city of Monopoli's fortress walls toward the toe of Italy's boot.